JENNIFER FAHNDRICH

THE WAY TO THE HEAVENLY BALL

Trilogy Christian Publishers

A Wholly Owned Subsidiary of Trinity Broadcasting Network

2442 Michelle Drive

Tustin, CA 92780

Copyright © 2023 by Jennifer Fahndrich

Scripture quotations marked NLT are taken from the Holy Bible, New Living Translation, copyright © 1996, 2004, 2015 by Tyndale House Foundation. Used by permission of Tyndale House Publishers, Inc., Carol Stream, Illinois 60188. All rights reserved.

All rights reserved, including the right to reproduce this book or portions thereof in any form whatsoever.

For information, address Trilogy Christian Publishing

Rights Department, 2442 Michelle Drive, Tustin, Ca 92780.

Trilogy Christian Publishing/ TBN and colophon are trademarks of Trinity Broadcasting Network.

For information about special discounts for bulk purchases, please contact Trilogy Christian Publishing.

Trilogy Disclaimer: The views and content expressed in this book are those of the author and may not necessarily reflect the views and doctrine of Trilogy Christian Publishing or the Trinity Broadcasting Network.

10 9 8 7 6 5 4 3 2 1

Library of Congress Cataloging-in-Publication Data is available.

B-ISBN 979-8-89041-266-9

E-ISBN 979-8-89042-267-6 (ebook)

"FOR THIS IS HOW GOD LOVED THE WORLD: HE GAVE HIS ONE AND ONLY SON, SO THAT EVERYONE WHO BELIEVES IN HIM WILL NOT PERISH BUT HAVE ETERNAL LIFE."

JOHN 3:16 (NEW LIVING TRANSLATION)

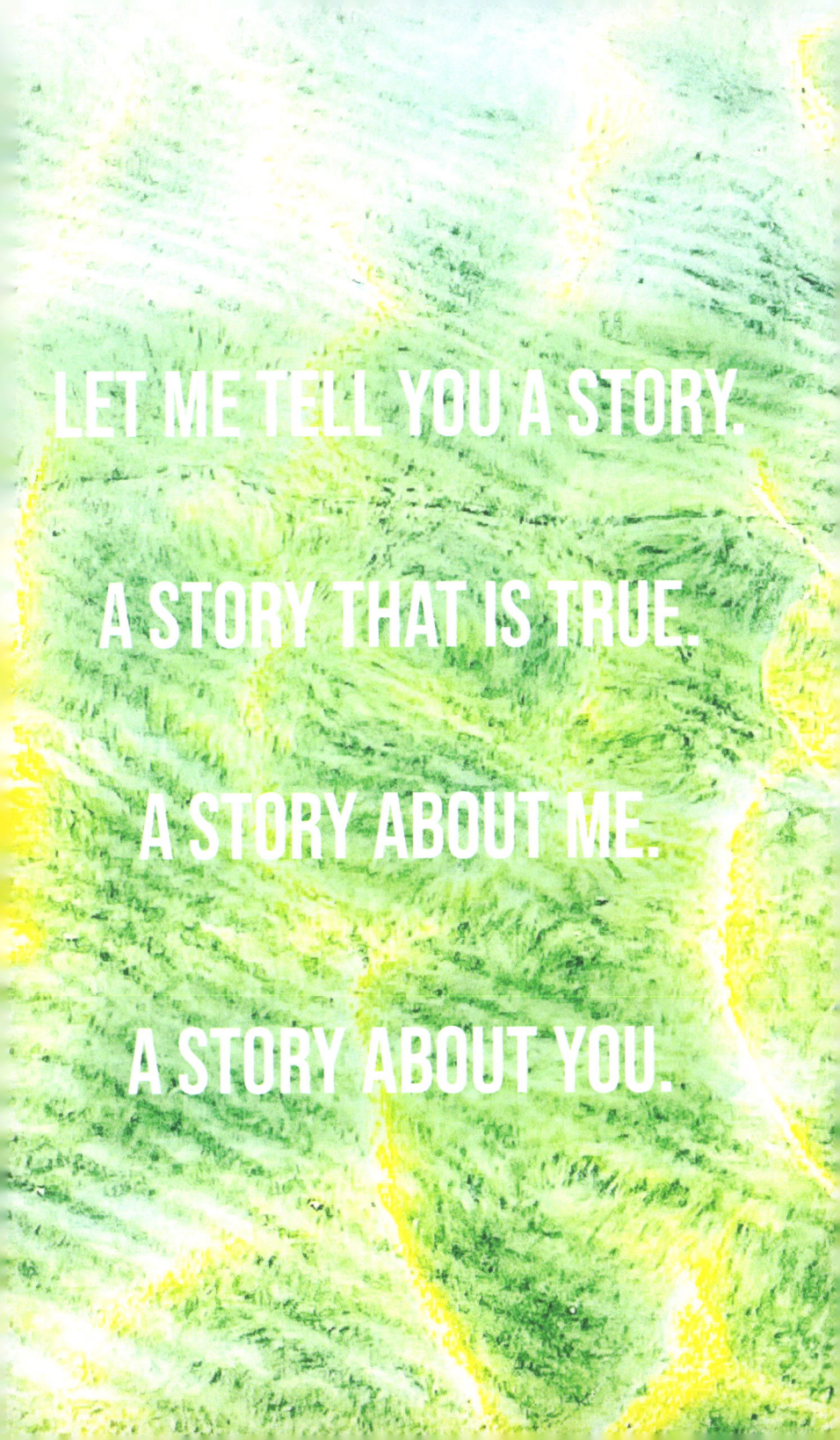

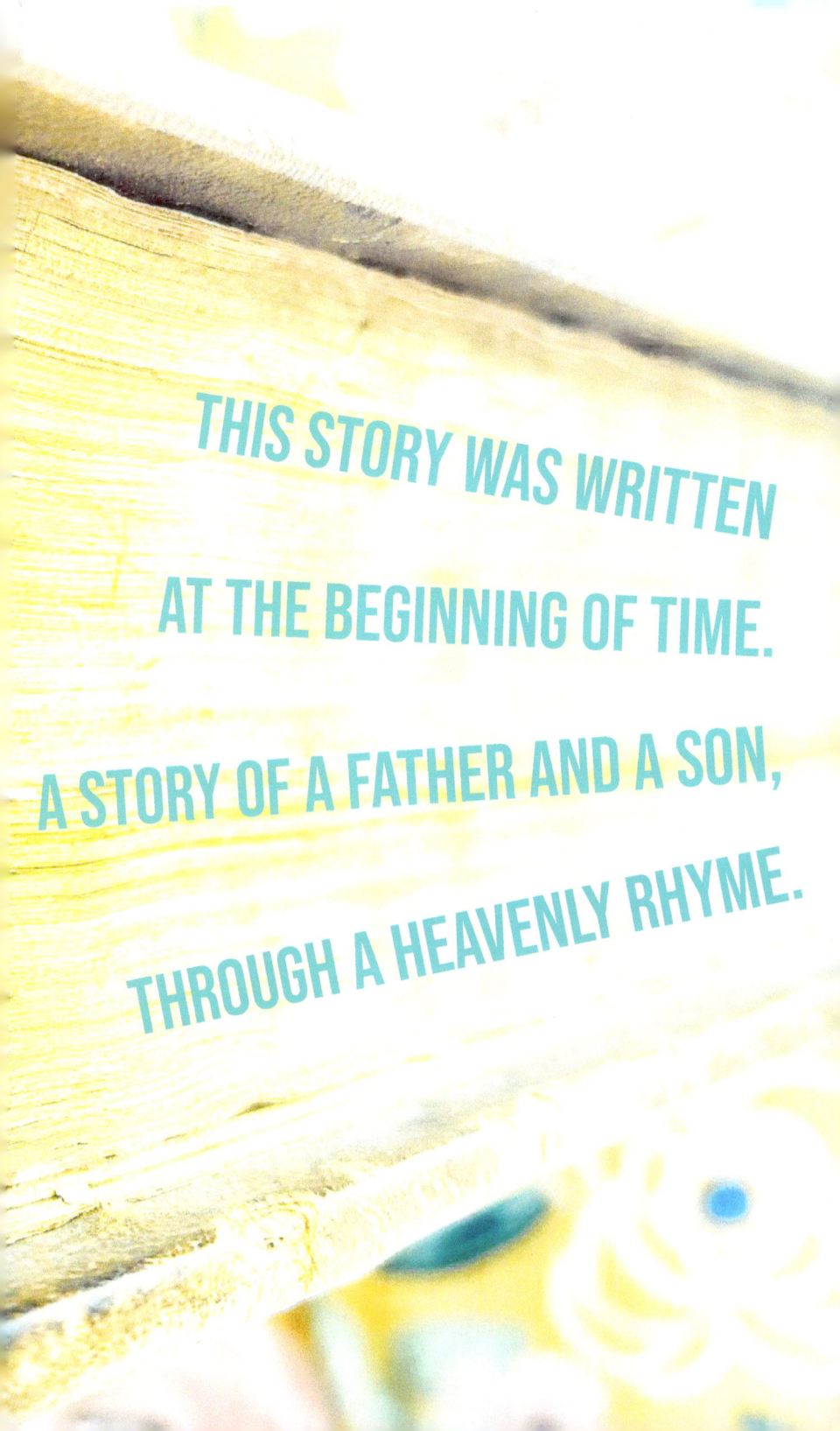

THIS STORY WAS WRITTEN

AT THE BEGINNING OF TIME.

A STORY OF A FATHER AND A SON,

THROUGH A HEAVENLY RHYME.

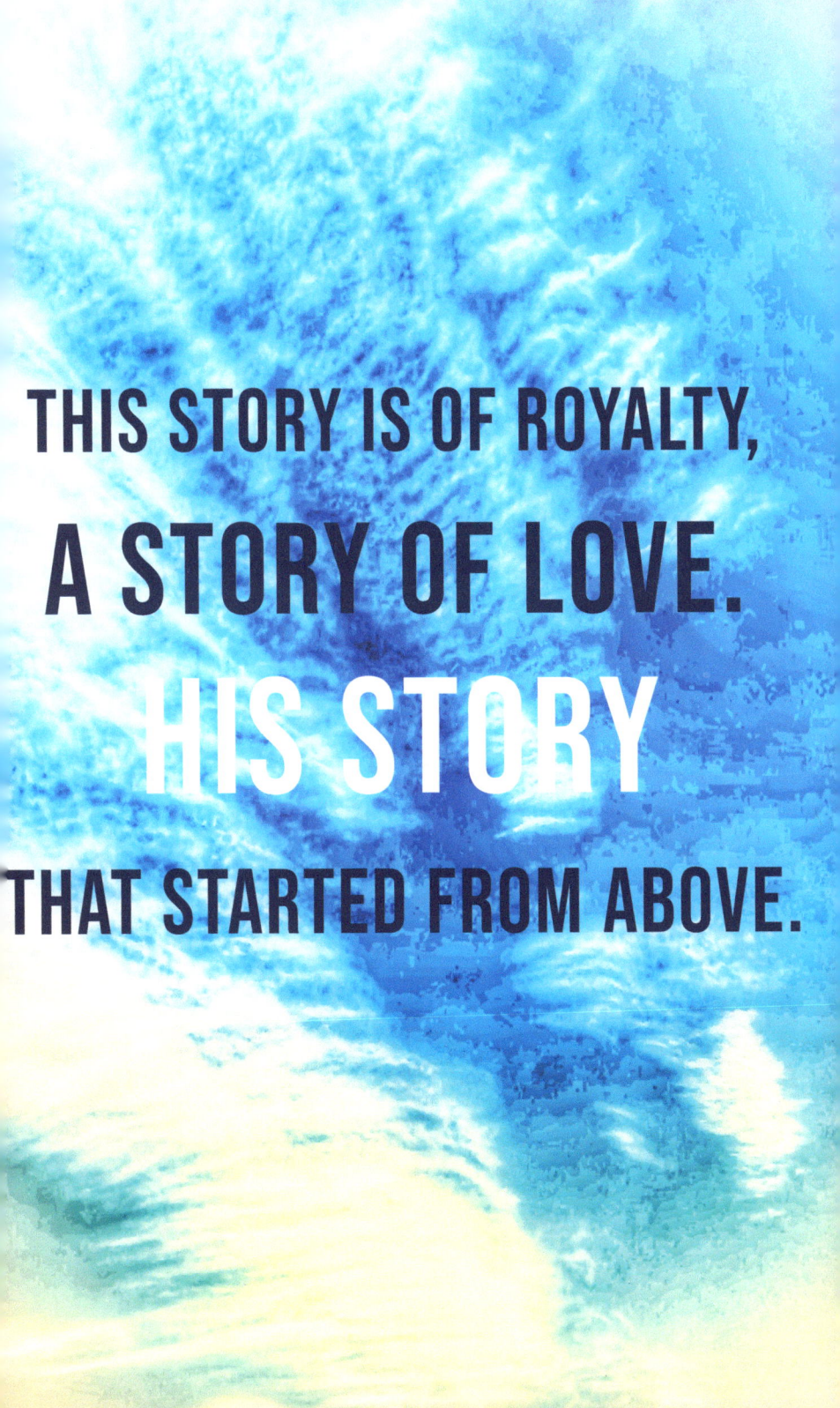

IT IS ABOUT A KING, HIS KINGDOM, AND WHAT OUR HEARTS DESIRE. **NOT JUST WORLDLY TREASURES TO ADMIRE.**

IT IS ALL ABOUT LOVE

IN THIS KINGDOM, YOU SEE!

THE GIFT OF THE HOLY SPIRIT

HAS BEEN GIVEN

FOR FREE!

GOD CREATED THE HEAVENS, AND ALSO THE EARTH.

JUST OPEN THE BIBLE, IT'S IN THE FIRST VERSE!

THE GLORY OF GOD

IS THE LIGHT THAT SHINES

IT IS FILLED WITH WONDERS

WE CAN'T IMAGINE

IN OUR MINDS!

ON EARTH, WE ALL JOURNEY IN OUR SLICE OF TIME.

GOD HAS WRITTEN ALL OUR STORIES AND CREATED US DIVINE.

THE BIBLE GIVES US HOPE FOR WHEN THESE EARTHLY JOURNEYS ARE DONE.

THERE IS A HEAVENLY CELEBRATION AWAITING

BECAUSE OF GOD'S ONE AND ONLY SON!

THESE LOVED ONES ARE NOT MISSING OR GHOSTLY OR GONE. THEY ARE ALIVE WITH THE LORD, JOYFULLY SINGING HIM SONGS!

THEY ARE MORE VIBRANT THAN EVER!

IMAGINE THEIR JOYFUL ENDEAVORS!

THE KEY TO THE KINGDOM

IS SIMPLE, YOU SEE.

ALL THAT HE ASKS,

IS THAT YOU

BELIEVE.

BELIEVE IN THE KING,
THE ONE WE CALL
JESUS.
BELIEVE THAT HE DIED,
ROSE AGAIN,

AND HAS SAVED US!

ASK FOR YOUR SINS TO BE FORGIVEN. **GOD** WILL HEAR YOUR CALL.

YOU WILL BE MADE NEW THROUGH **JESUS**, WHO TAKES THEM ALL!

THE HOLY SPIRIT WILL COME

AS A GIFT FILLED WITH LOVE.

WHEN YOU ASK,

HE WILL

FIT YOUR HEART
LIKE A GLOVE.

IT'S WHAT HE DID FOR ME AND WHAT HE DID FOR YOU! OUR PERFECT KING CAME TO CARRY US THROUGH!

TRUST IN HIS TRUTH,
THROUGH JESUS, YOU ARE FREE,

BASED ON THE VERSE
OF JOHN 3:16.

THE KEY TO THE KINGDOM IS <u>HIM</u>,
NOT YOU OR ME.

IT IS NOT WORKS,

OR KINDNESS OR CARE.

ALTHOUGH, THESE ARE GREAT

WAYS TO LIVE WELL

AND BE FAIR.

ON EARTH WE HAVE FREE WILL

AND WE TRY TO BE TOUGH.

IN HEAVEN, OUR EFFORT?...

IT'S JUST
NOT ENOUGH!

THE DOOR
THAT YOU ENTER
ONLY NEEDS ONE THING,
A DECISION FROM YOU TO FOLLOW
JESUS THE KING.

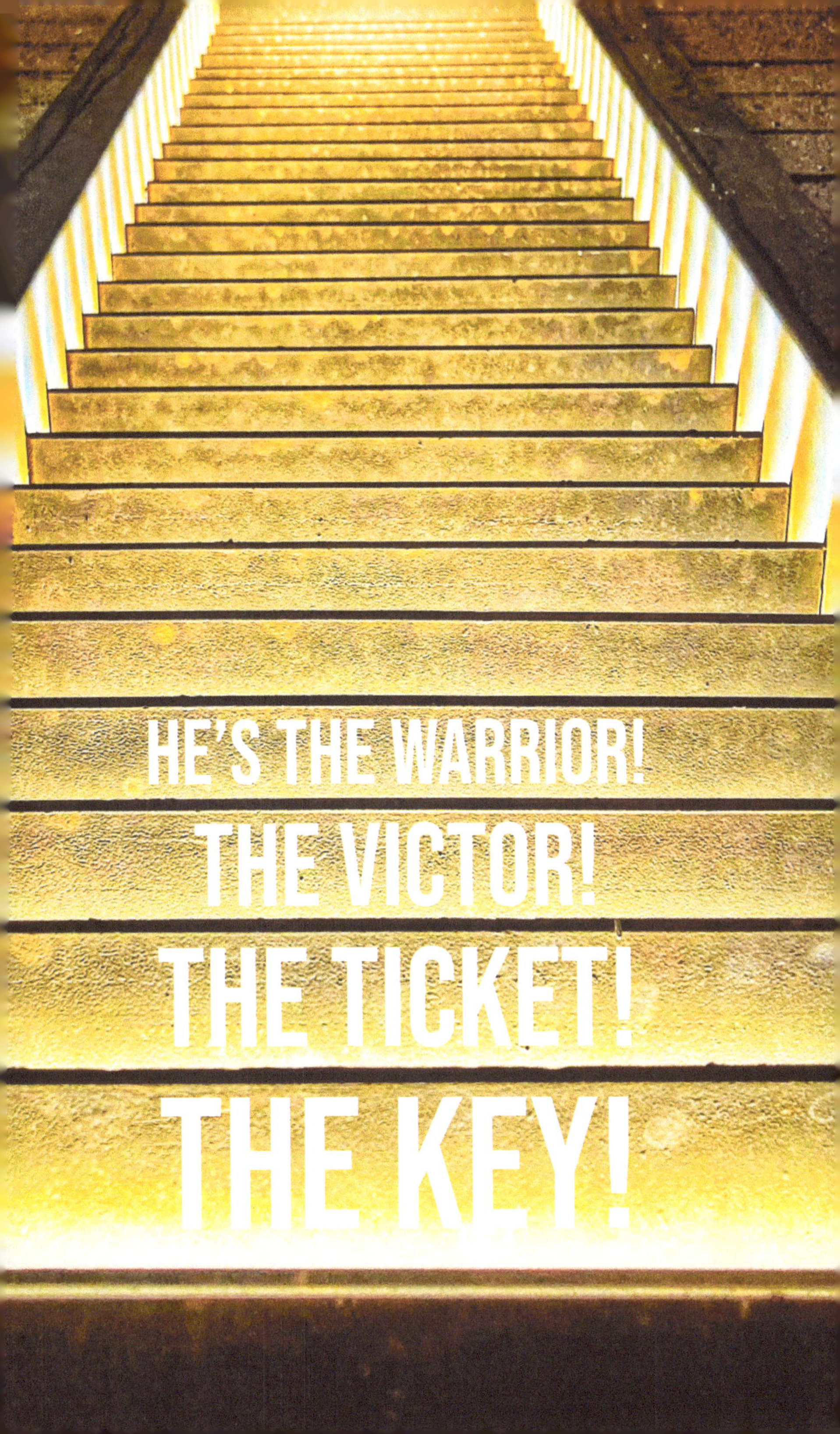
HE'S THE WARRIOR!
THE VICTOR!
THE TICKET!
THE KEY!

HE'S THE ONE WHO DIED FOR YOU!

HE'S THE ONE WHO DIED FOR ME!

DON'T MISS YOUR CHANCE TO GO TO THE BALL!

YOUR TIME ON EARTH COULD BE LONG...

**BUT FOR OTHERS,
IT HAS ALSO BEEN SMALL.**

IF YOU BELIEVE, THEN YOU WILL RECEIVE!
AS YOU ARE BUSY HERE ON EARTH, PLEASE
LISTEN TO HIS CALL!

THE KING IS THE WAY TO THE HEAVENLY BALL.

AMEN.

Printed in the USA
CPSIA information can be obtained
at www.ICGtesting.com
LVHW070440091123
763416LV00001B/1